Name _______________

Draw a Picture

I Can...

- [ ] use a Capital Letter
  <u>T</u>he cat is big.
- [ ] use spaces
- [ ] sound out words
  d-o-g = dog
- [ ] use a Period .
- [ ] Draw a picture

He is having fun, running under the sun with his new toy gun.

fun	gun	run	sun
zabawa	pistolet	biegać	słońce

Name: ______________________ Date: ______________________

Today is: Monday | Tuesday | Wednesday | Thursday | Friday

Direction: Trace and read the sentences.

bag	rag	tag	wag

torba	szmata	etykietka	machanie

He has many bags.

I see a rag.

I see a tag.

Its tail is wagging.

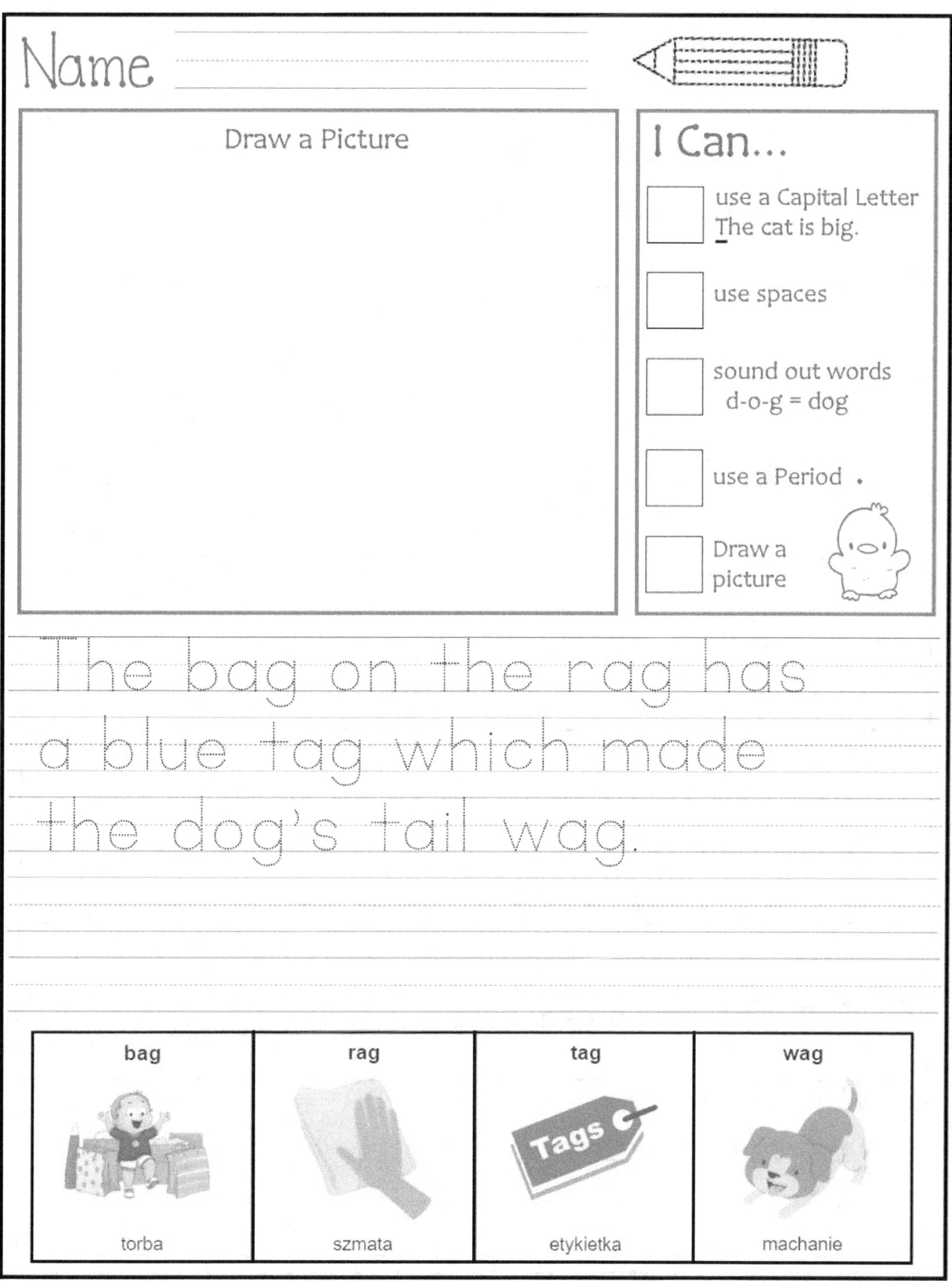

Name
Draw a Picture
I Can...
use a Capital Letter
The cat is big.
use spaces
sound out words
d-o-g = dog
use a Period .
Draw a picture
The bag on the rag has a blue tag which made the dog's tail wag.
bag
torba
rag
szmata
tag
etykietka
wag
machanie

Name: _________________ Date: _______________

Today is: [Monday] [Tuesday] [Wednesday]
[Thursday] [Friday]

Direction: Trace and read the sentences.

can	**man**	**pan**	**van**
puszki	mężczyzna	patelnia	awangarda

I see a can of soda.

The man is happy.

The pan is dirty.

I see a big van.

Draw a Picture

I Can...

- [ ] use a Capital Letter
  <u>T</u>he cat is big.
- [ ] use spaces
- [ ] sound out words
  d-o-g = dog
- [ ] use a Period .
- [ ] Draw a picture

The man who was driving a van ran over a can and a pan.

can	man	pan	van
puszki	mężczyzna	patelnia	awangarda

Name: ______________________ Date: ____________________

Today is: Monday Tuesday Wednesday Thursday Friday

Direction: Trace and read the sentences.

cut	gut	hut	nut

skaleczenie	jelito	chata	orzech

He cut his nails.

He has a gut.

This is a small hut.

It is holding a nut.

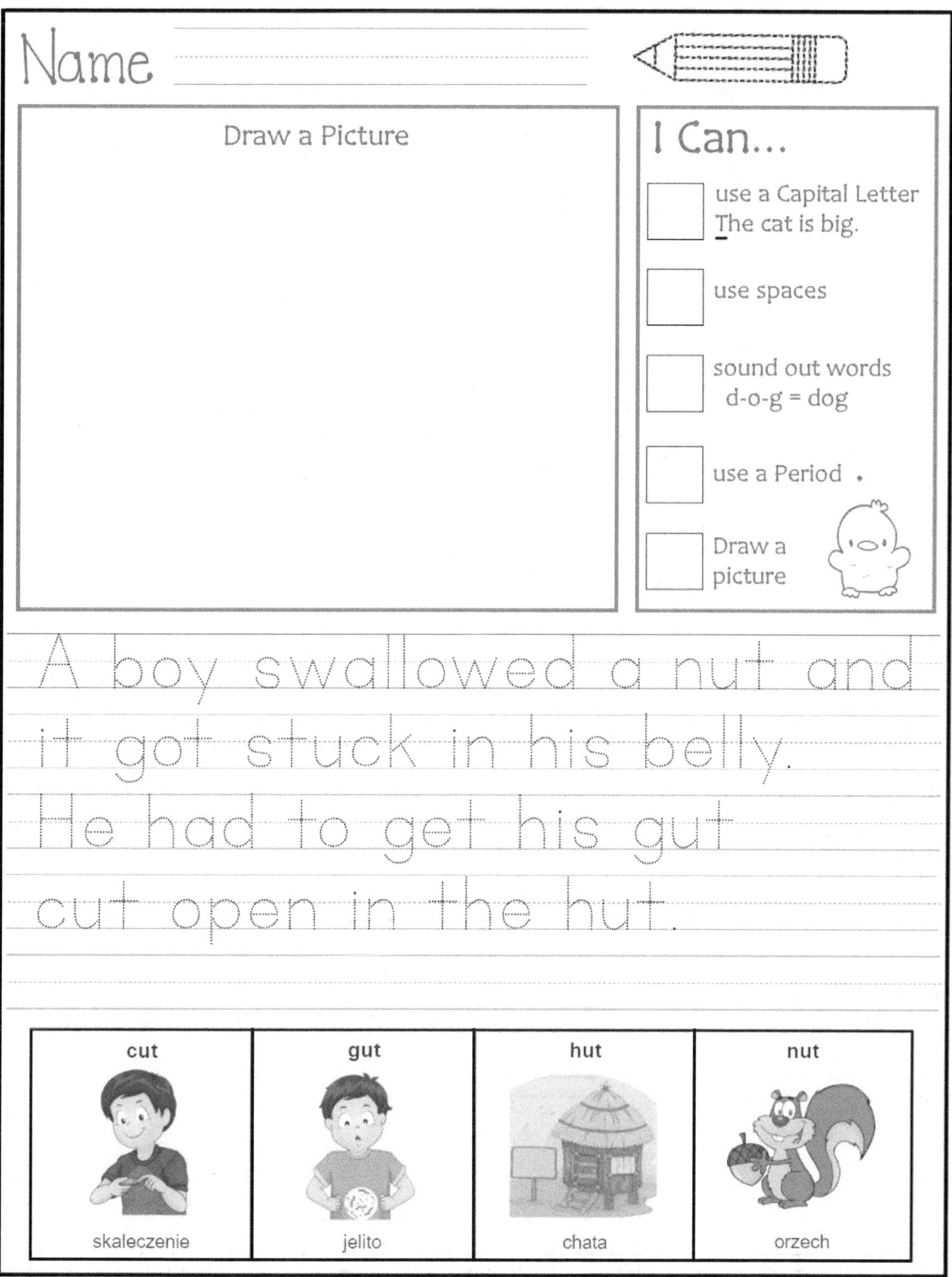

Name

Draw a Picture

I Can...

use a Capital Letter
The cat is big.

use spaces

sound out words
d-o-g = dog

use a Period .

Draw a
picture

A boy swallowed a nut and
it got stuck in his belly.
He had to get his gut
cut open in the hut.

cut
skaleczenie

gut
jelito

hut
chata

nut
orzech

Name: _________________________ Date: _______________

Today is: Monday   Tuesday   Wednesday   Thursday   Friday

Direction: Trace and read the sentences.

fat	cat	hat	mat
gruby	kot	kapelusz	mata

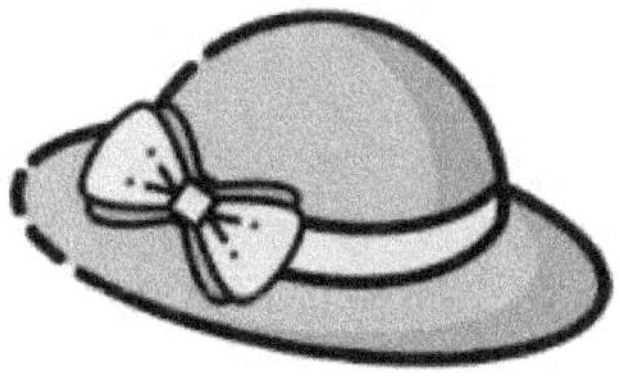

I see a fat dog.

This is my little cat.

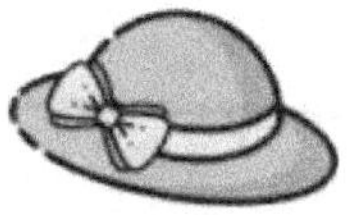

I like this hat.

I see a big mat.

Draw a Picture

I Can...

- [ ] use a Capital Letter
  The cat is big.

- [ ] use spaces

- [ ] sound out words
  d-o-g = dog

- [ ] use a Period .

- [ ] Draw a picture

The fat cat laid on the mat that was a hat pattern.

fat	cat	hat	mat
gruby	kot	kapelusz	mata

Name: _________________________ Date: _______________

Today is: Monday Tuesday Wednesday Thursday Friday

Direction: Trace and read the sentences.

cab	lab	tab	crab
taksówka	laboratorium	patka	krab

The cab is fast.

The lab is exciting.

The tab is long.

We found a crab.

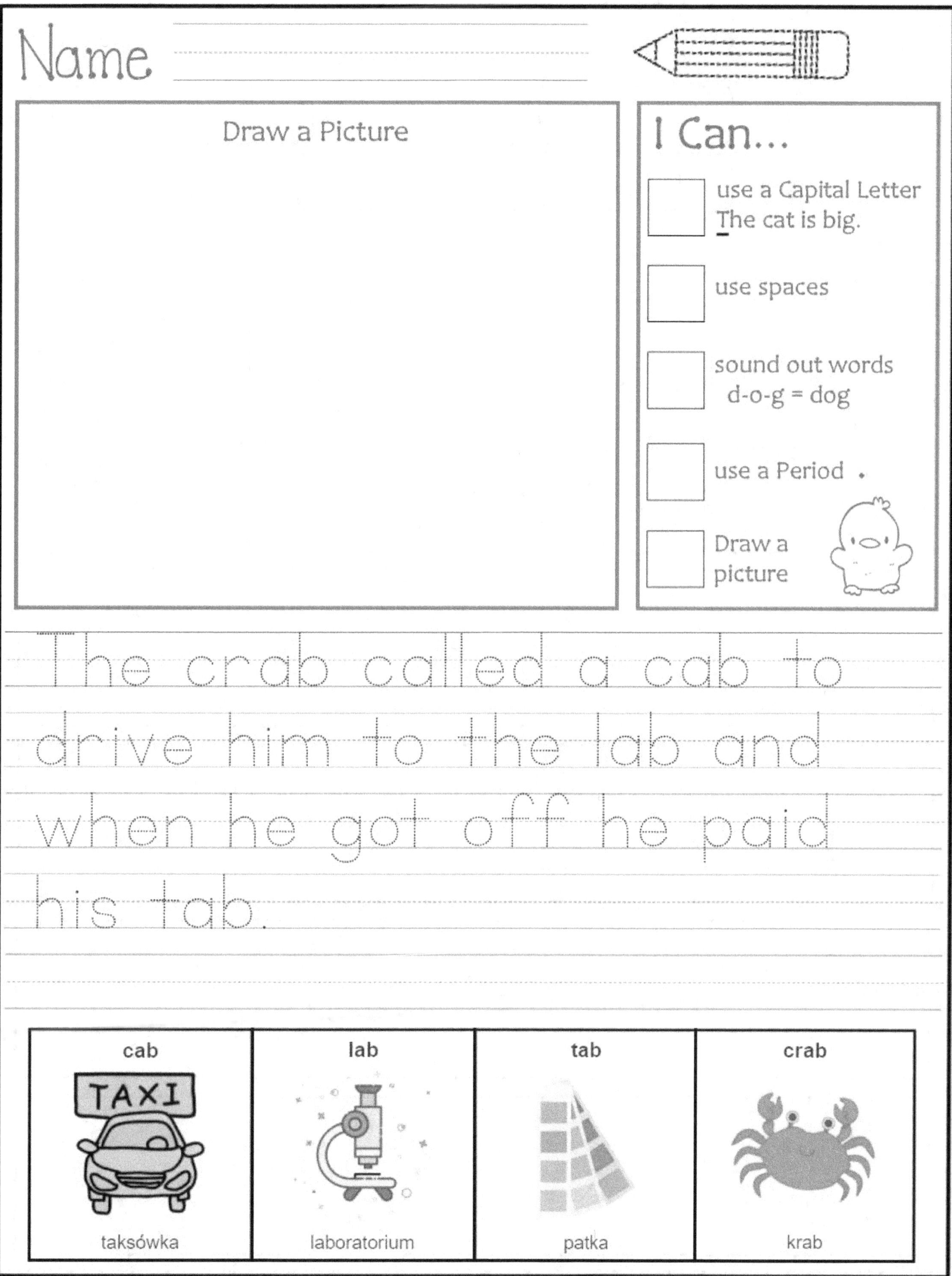

Name
Draw a Picture
I Can...
use a Capital Letter
The cat is big.
use spaces
sound out words
d-o-g = dog
use a Period .
Draw a
picture
The crab called a cab to drive him to the lab and when he got off he paid his tab.
cab
TAXI
taksówka
lab
laboratorium
tab
patka
crab
krab

Name: ______________________ Date: ______________________

Today is: [Monday] [Tuesday] [Wednesday]
           [Thursday] [Friday]

Direction: Trace and read the sentences.

ham	jam	ram	clam
szynka	dżem	owca	muszla

I like to eat ham.

We like to eat jam.

The ram is big.

The clam is pretty.

Name _______________

Draw a Picture

I Can...

☐ use a Capital Letter
The cat is big.

☐ use spaces

☐ sound out words
d-o-g = dog

☐ use a Period .

☐ Draw a picture

The clam gave the ram ham. Then the ram gave the clam jam.

ham	jam	ram	clam
szynka	dżem	owca	muszla

Name: ______________________ Date: ______________________

Today is: Monday | Tuesday | Wednesday | Thursday | Friday

Direction: Trace and read the sentences.

bed	led	red	wed
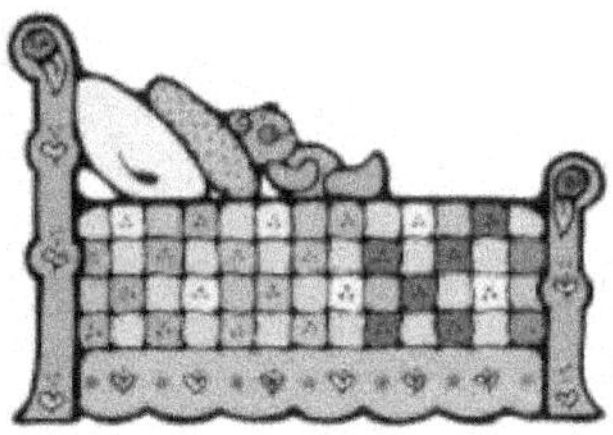			
łóżko	prowadzący	czerwony	ślub

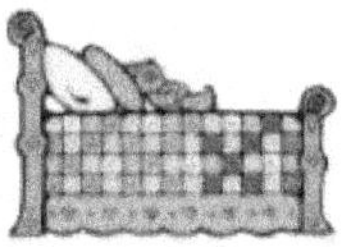

This is my little bed.

He led us to safety.

The apple is red.

He asks her to wed.

Draw a Picture

I Can...

- [ ] use a Capital Letter
  The cat is big.
- [ ] use spaces
- [ ] sound out words
  d-o-g = dog
- [ ] use a Period .
- [ ] Draw a picture

When the prince got out of bed, he was led on a red carpet to be wed with the princess.

bed	led	red	wed
łóżko	prowadzący	czerwony	ślub

Name: _______________________ Date: _______________

Today is: [Monday] [Tuesday] [Wednesday] [Thursday] [Friday]

Direction: Trace and read the sentences.

bad	dad	mad	sad
zły	tata	szalony	smutny

This apple is bad.

My dad is very kind.

The reindeer is mad.

The little cat is sad.

Name

Draw a Picture

I Can...

- [ ] use a Capital Letter
  The cat is big.
- [ ] use spaces
- [ ] sound out words
  d-o-g = dog
- [ ] use a Period .
- [ ] Draw a picture

I was bad so my dad
got mad and now
I am so sad.

bad	**dad**	**mad**	**sad**

zły	tata	szalony	smutny

Name: _________________ Date: _______________

Today is: Monday Tuesday Wednesday
           Thursday Friday

Direction: Trace and read the sentences.

den	**hen**	**pen**	**ten**
legowisko	kura	stajnie	dziesięć

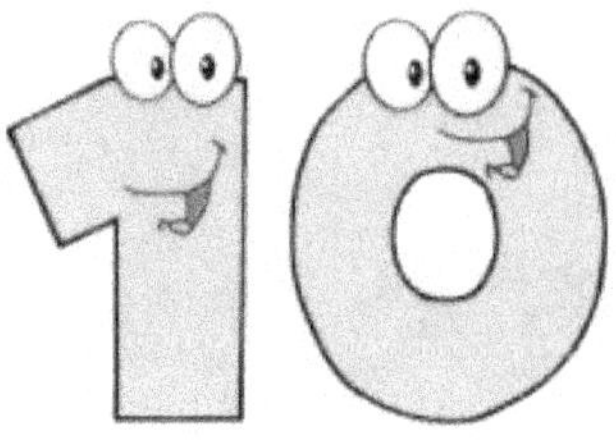

It is a den.

The hens lay eggs.

She has a good pen.

The ten is smiling.

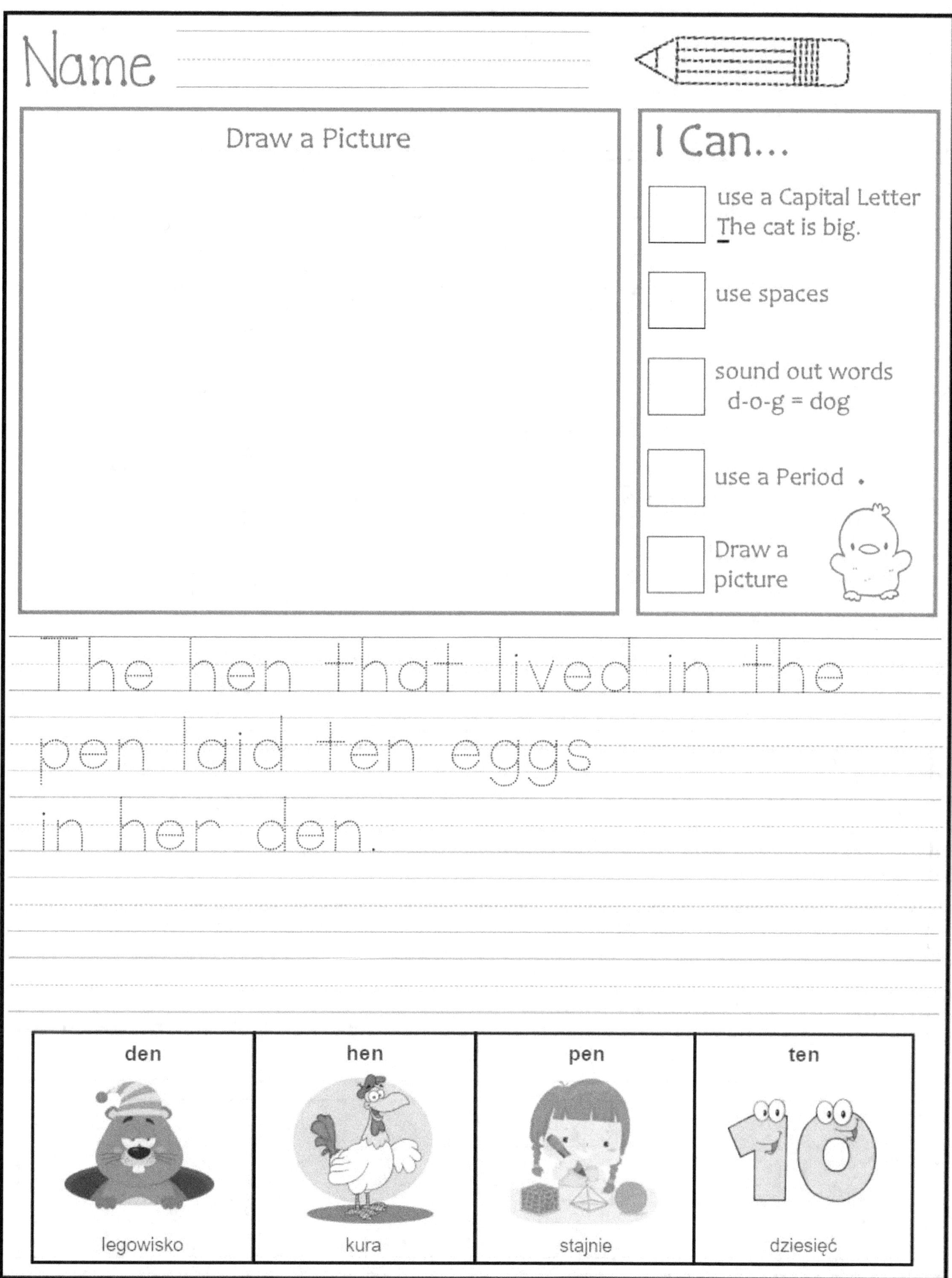

Name

Draw a Picture

I Can...

use a Capital Letter
The cat is big.

use spaces

sound out words
d-o-g = dog

use a Period .

Draw a
picture

The hen that lived in the
pen laid ten eggs
in her den.

den
legowisko

hen
kura

pen
stajnie

ten
dziesięć

Name: _________________ Date: _________________

Today is: [Monday] [Tuesday] [Wednesday]
[Thursday] [Friday]

Direction: Trace and read the sentences.

gum	mum	sum	drum
lepki	milczący	suma	bęben

I like to chew gum.

My mum is kind!

I can do a sum!

The drum is big.

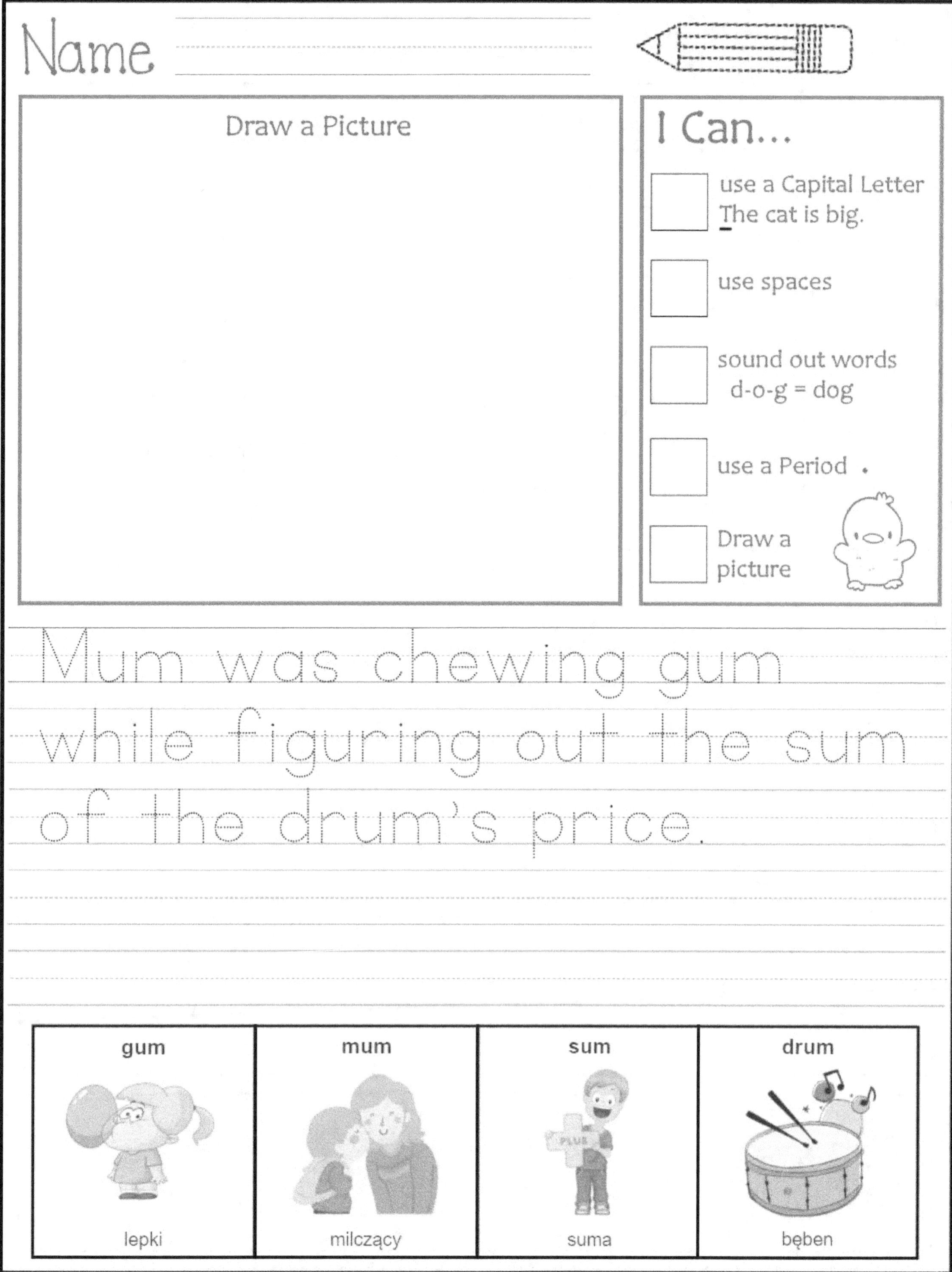

Name

Draw a Picture

I Can...

use a Capital Letter
The cat is big.

use spaces

sound out words
d-o-g = dog

use a Period .

Draw a
picture

Mum was chewing gum while figuring out the sum of the drum's price.

gum
lepki

mum
milczący

sum
suma

drum
bęben

Name: _________________________ Date: _________________________

Today is: Monday Tuesday Wednesday Thursday Friday

Direction: Trace and read the sentences.

bid	hid	kid	lid
stawka	ukryć	dziecko	pokrywa

He likes to bid.

He is hiding.

The kid like to play.

I see a lid.

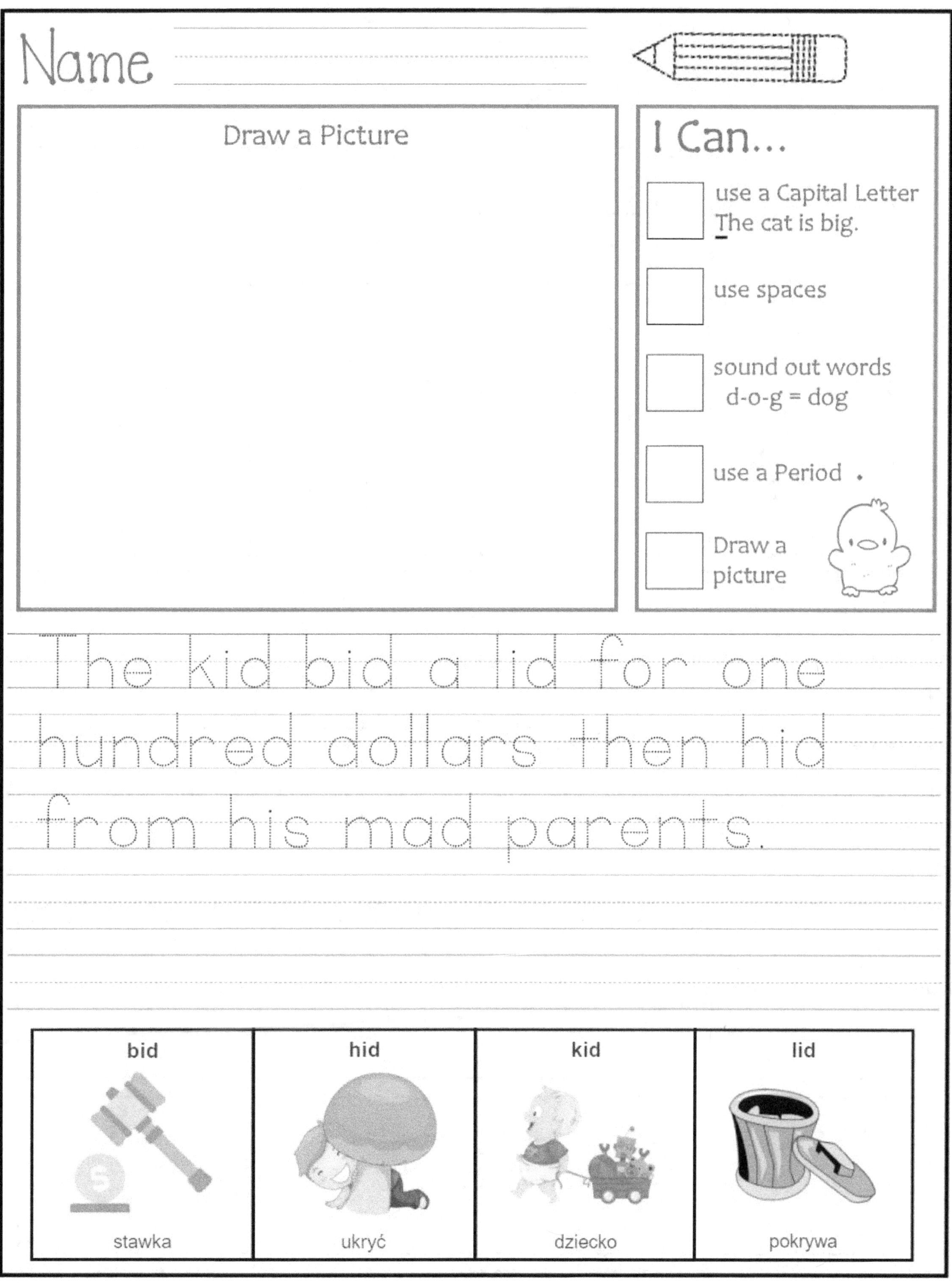

Name

Draw a Picture

I Can...

- [ ] use a Capital Letter
  The cat is big.

- [ ] use spaces

- [ ] sound out words
  d-o-g = dog

- [ ] use a Period .

- [ ] Draw a picture

The kid bid a lid for one hundred dollars then hid from his mad parents.

bid	hid	kid	lid
stawka	ukryć	dziecko	pokrywa

Name: ___________________ Date: ___________________

Today is: [Monday] [Tuesday] [Wednesday]
[Thursday] [Friday]

Direction: Trace and read the sentences.

big	**dig**	**pig**	**wig**
duży	kopać	świnia	peruka

That is a big pencil.

He will dig up a hole.

The pig is fat.

She puts on a wig.

Draw a Picture

I Can...

- [ ] use a Capital Letter
  The cat is big.
- [ ] use spaces
- [ ] sound out words
  d-o-g = dog
- [ ] use a Period .
- [ ] Draw a picture

The big pig went to dig
in the mud for his wig.

big	**dig**	**pig**	**wig**
duży	kopać	świnia	peruka

Name: _________________ Date: _______________

Today is: Monday   Tuesday   Wednesday
           Thursday   Friday

Direction: Trace and read the sentences.

bin	fin	pin	win
kosz	płetwa	kołek	zdobyć

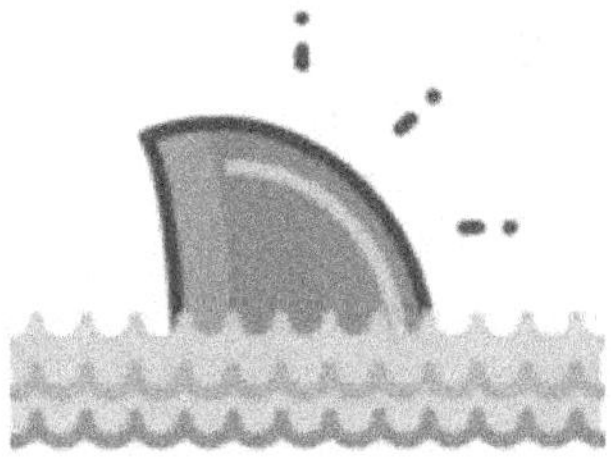

It is a recycle bin.

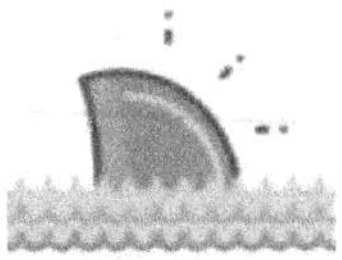

The shark has a fin.

The pin is pointy.

He won the match.

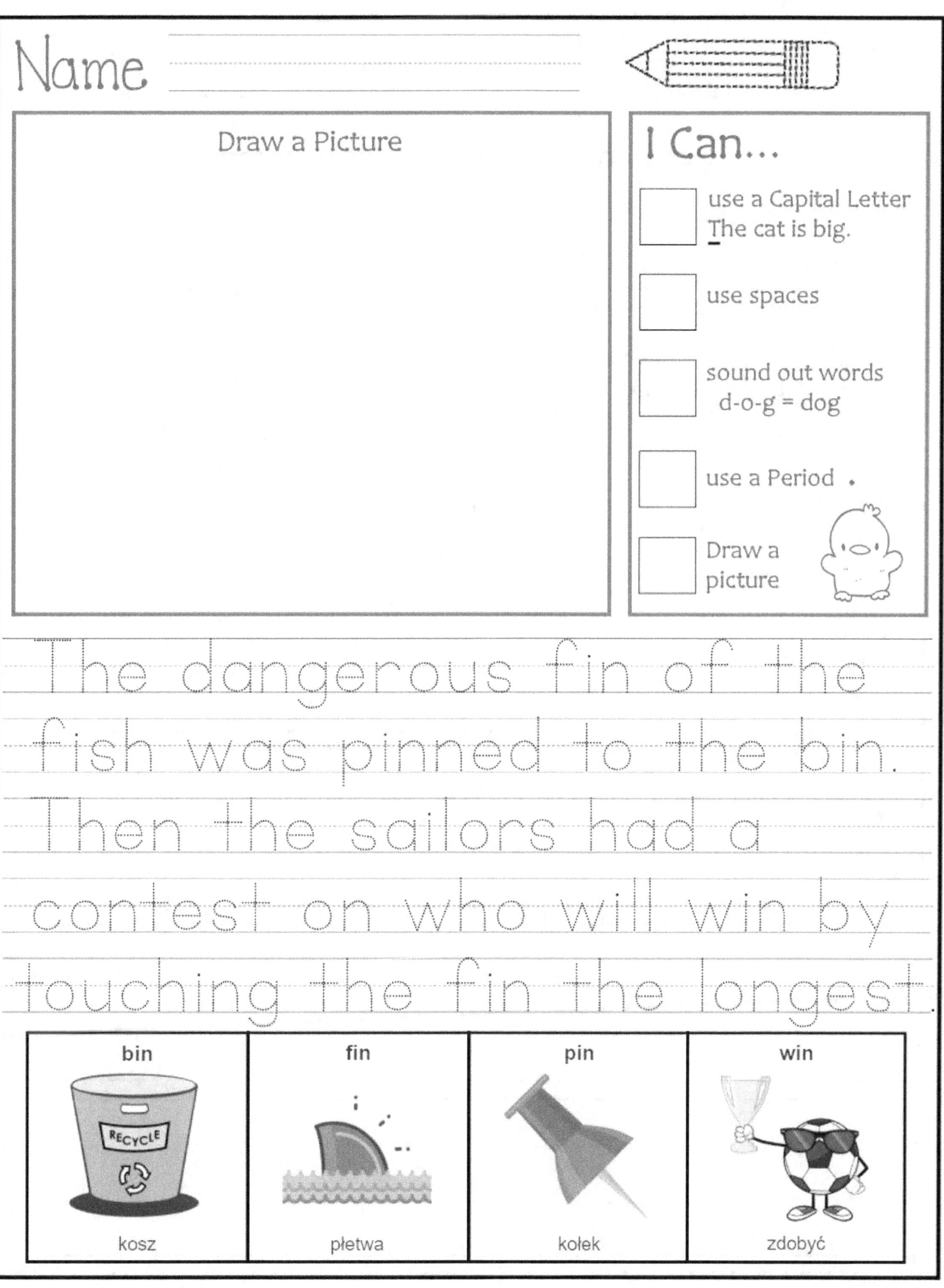

Name

Draw a Picture

I Can...

use a Capital Letter
The cat is big.

use spaces

sound out words
d-o-g = dog

use a Period .

Draw a
picture

The dangerous fin of the
fish was pinned to the bin.
Then the sailors had a
contest on who will win by
touching the fin the longest.

bin
RECYCLE
kosz

fin
płetwa

pin
kołek

win
zdobyć

Name: _____________ Date: _____________

Today is: Monday Tuesday Wednesday

Thursday Friday

Direction: Trace and read the sentences.

hip	lip	nip	sip
cześć p	usta	uszczypnięcie	drink

This is my hip.

Her lips are red.

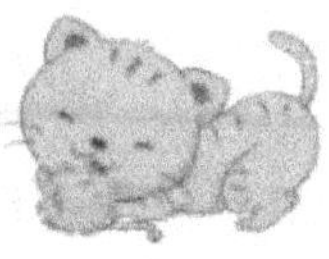

It is nipping its toy.

She is sipping.

Name

Draw a Picture

I Can...

- [ ] use a Capital Letter
  The cat is big.

- [ ] use spaces

- [ ] sound out words
  d-o-g = dog

- [ ] use a Period .

- [ ] Draw a picture

The dog nipped someone who was sipping water with his lip.

hip	lip	nip	sip
cześć p	usta	uszczypnięcie	drink

Name: _________________________ Date: _________________________

Today is: Monday Tuesday Wednesday Thursday Friday

Direction: Trace and read the sentences.

fit	hit	kit	sit
dopasowanie	trafienie	zestaw	siedzieć

It is perfectly fit.

They hit each other.

That is a safety kit.

He is sitting.

Draw a Picture

I Can...

- [ ] use a Capital Letter
  The cat is big.
- [ ] use spaces
- [ ] sound out words
  d-o-g = dog
- [ ] use a Period .
- [ ] Draw a picture

The fit doctor sat then was hit by a kit.

fit	hit	kit	sit
dopasowanie	trafienie	zestaw	siedzieć

Name: ______________________ Date: ______________________

Today is: Monday | Tuesday | Wednesday | Thursday | Friday

Direction: Trace and read the sentences.

cob	job	rob	sob

kukurydza	praca	obrabować	płakać

I ate corn on the cob.

This is my job.

He is robbing.

The girl is sobbing.

Draw a Picture

The chef robbed a corn
cob and then was sobbing
because he had lost his
job.

cob	job	rob	sob
kukurydza	praca	obrabować	płakać

Name: _________________________ Date: _________________

Today is: [Monday] [Tuesday] [Wednesday]
[Thursday] [Friday]

Direction: Trace and read the sentences.

dog	hog	jog	log
pies	wieprz	jogging	drewno

The dog is thrilled.

The hog is big.

She is jogging.

The log is small.

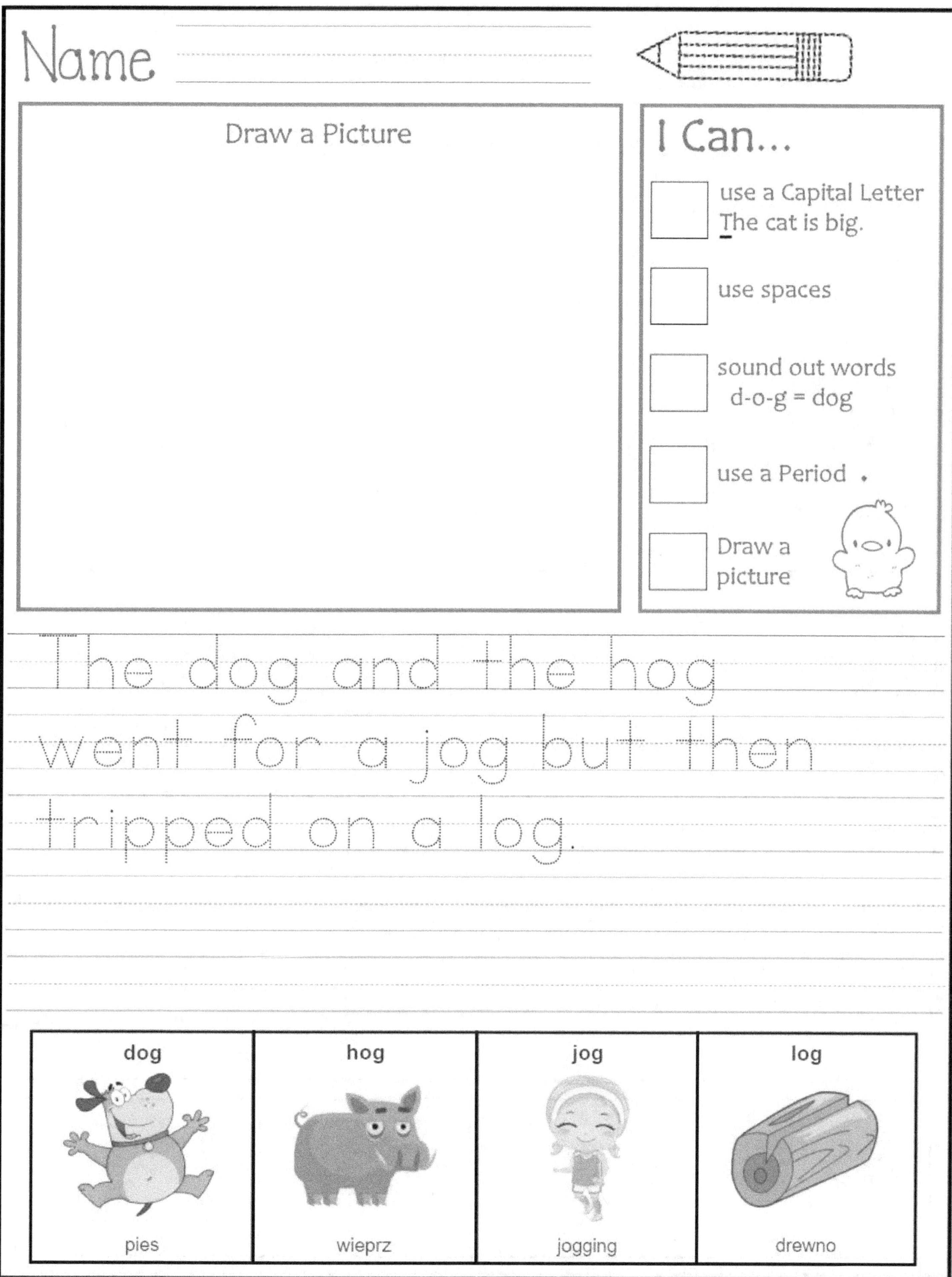

Name

Draw a Picture

I Can...

- [ ] use a Capital Letter
  The cat is big.

- [ ] use spaces

- [ ] sound out words
  d-o-g = dog

- [ ] use a Period .

- [ ] Draw a picture

The dog and the hog went for a jog but then tripped on a log.

dog	hog	jog	log
pies	wieprz	jogging	drewno

Name: ______________________ Date: ______________

Today is: [Monday] [Tuesday] [Wednesday]
           [Thursday] [Friday]

Direction: Trace and read the sentences.

bug	hug	jug	mug
pluskwa	przytulić	dzbanek	kubek

The bug is colorful.

She is hugging.

The jug has milk in it.

He has a mug.

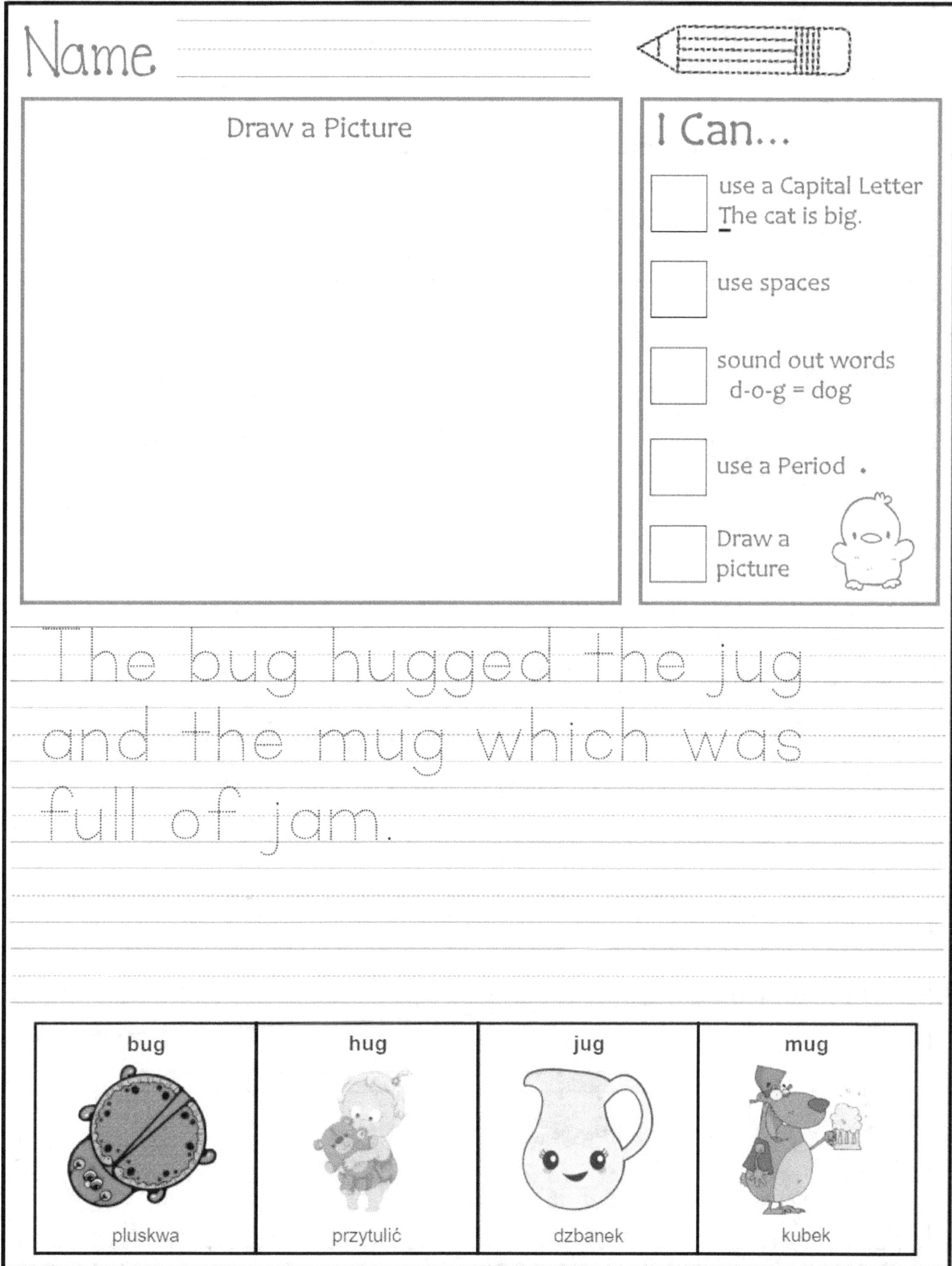

Name

Draw a Picture

I Can...

use a Capital Letter
The cat is big.

use spaces

sound out words
d-o-g = dog

use a Period .

Draw a
picture

The bug hugged the jug
and the mug which was
full of jam.

bug
pluskwa

hug
przytulić

jug
dzbanek

mug
kubek

Name: ______________________ Date: ______________________

Today is: Monday Tuesday Wednesday Thursday Friday

Direction: Trace and read the sentences.

cot	dot	hot	pot

łóżko	kropka	gorąco	garnek

This is my cot.

There are many dots.

It is very hot.

He has a plant pot.

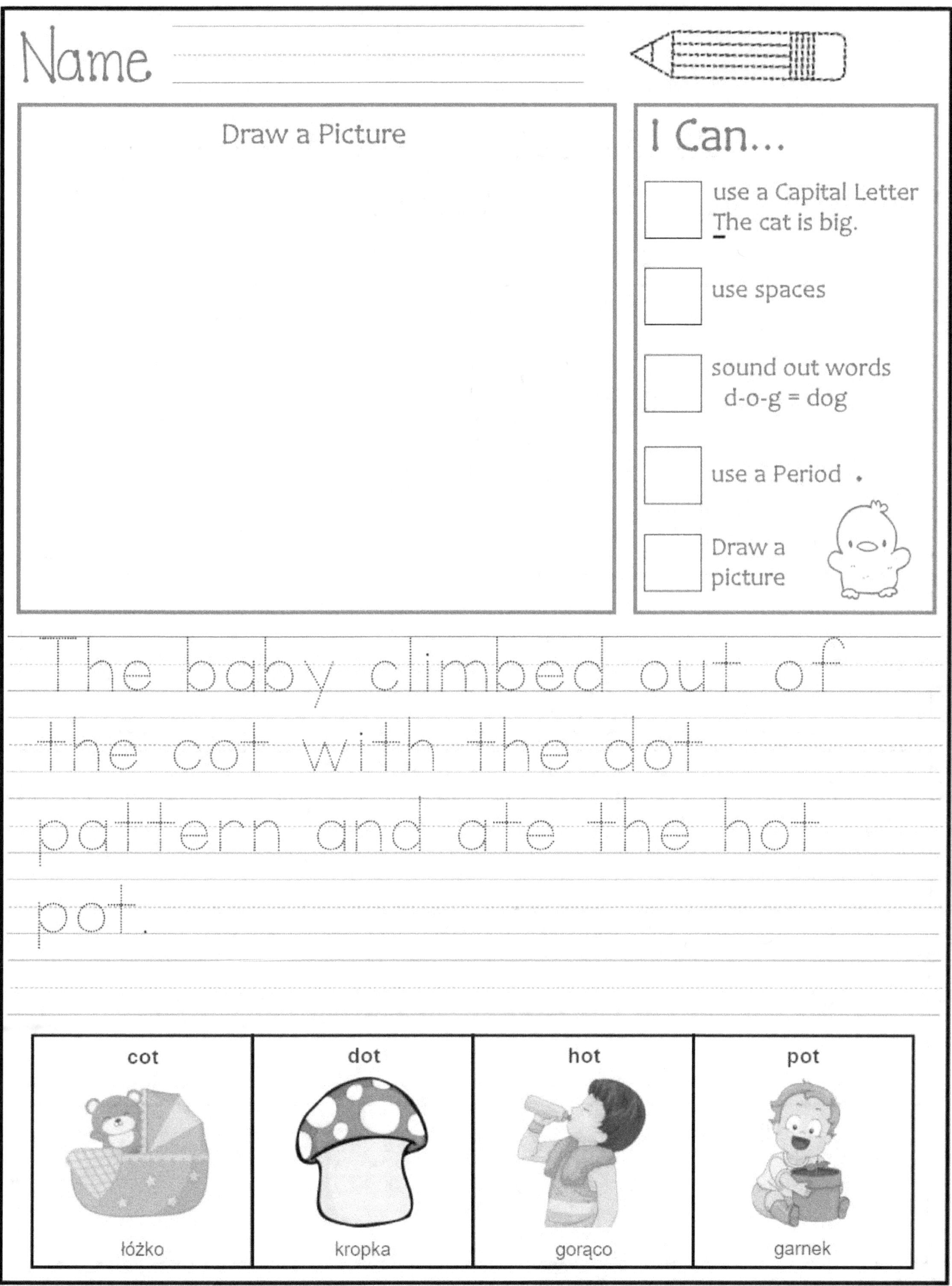

The baby climbed out of the cot with the dot pattern and ate the hot pot.

cot	dot	hot	pot
łóżko	kropka	gorąco	garnek

Name: ___________________ Date: ___________________

Today is: Monday Tuesday Wednesday
Thursday Friday

Direction: Read the words and make a sentence.

fun	gun	run	sun
zabawa	pistolet	biegać	słońce

Name

Draw a Picture

I Can...

- [ ] use a Capital Letter
  The cat is big.

- [ ] use spaces

- [ ] sound out words
  d-o-g = dog

- [ ] use a Period .

- [ ] Draw a picture

Name: _______________________ Date: _______________________

Today is: Monday   Tuesday   Wednesday
          Thursday   Friday

Name: _______________________ Date: _______________________

Today is: [Monday] [Tuesday] [Wednesday]
[Thursday] [Friday]

Direction: Read the words and make a sentence.

bag	**rag**	**tag**	**wag**
torba	szmata	etykietka	machanie

Name

Draw a Picture

I Can...

- [ ] use a Capital Letter
  The cat is big.

- [ ] use spaces

- [ ] sound out words
  d-o-g = dog

- [ ] use a Period .

- [ ] Draw a picture

Name: _____________________ Date: _____________________

Today is: Monday Tuesday Wednesday
Thursday Friday

Name: _________________________ Date: _________________________

Today is: [Monday] [Tuesday] [Wednesday]
[Thursday] [Friday]

Direction: Read the words and make a sentence.

can	**man**	**pan**	**van**
puszki	mężczyzna	patelnia	awangarda

Draw a Picture

I Can...

- ☐ use a Capital Letter
  The cat is big.

- ☐ use spaces

- ☐ sound out words
  d-o-g = dog

- ☐ use a Period .

- ☐ Draw a picture

Name: _______________________ Date: _______________________

Today is: Monday Tuesday Wednesday Thursday Friday

Name: _________________________ Date: _________________________

Today is: Monday | Tuesday | Wednesday

Thursday | Friday

Direction: Read the words and make a sentence.

cut	gut	hut	nut
skaleczenie	jelito	chata	orzech

Name

Draw a Picture

I Can...

- [ ] use a Capital Letter
  The cat is big.

- [ ] use spaces

- [ ] sound out words
  d-o-g = dog

- [ ] use a Period .

- [ ] Draw a picture

Name: _______________ Date: _______________

Today is: Monday Tuesday Wednesday

Thursday Friday

Name: _________________________ Date: _________________

Today is: Monday   Tuesday   Wednesday

Thursday   Friday

Direction: Read the words and make a sentence.

fat	cat	hat	mat
gruby	kot	kapelusz	mata

Name

Draw a Picture

I Can...

- [ ] use a Capital Letter
  The cat is big.

- [ ] use spaces

- [ ] sound out words
  d-o-g = dog

- [ ] use a Period .

- [ ] Draw a picture

Name: _____________________   Date: _____________________

Today is: Monday Tuesday Wednesday Thursday Friday

Name: _______________ Date: _______________

Today is: [Monday] [Tuesday] [Wednesday]
[Thursday] [Friday]

Direction: Read the words and make a sentence.

cab	lab	tab	crab
taksówka	laboratorium	patka	krab

Name

Draw a Picture

I Can...

☐ use a Capital Letter
The cat is big.

☐ use spaces

☐ sound out words
d-o-g = dog

☐ use a Period .

☐ Draw a picture

Name: _______________________   Date: _______________

Today is: [Monday] [Tuesday] [Wednesday]
          [Thursday] [Friday]

Name: _________________ Date: _______________

Today is: Monday Tuesday Wednesday Thursday Friday

Direction: Read the words and make a sentence.

ham	jam	ram	clam
szynka	dżem	owca	muszla

Name

Draw a Picture

I Can...

- ☐ use a Capital Letter
  The cat is big.

- ☐ use spaces

- ☐ sound out words
  d-o-g = dog

- ☐ use a Period .

- ☐ Draw a picture

Name: _________________________ Date: _________________

Today is: Monday   Tuesday   Wednesday

Thursday   Friday

Name: _________________________ Date: _________________________

Today is: [Monday] [Tuesday] [Wednesday]
[Thursday] [Friday]

Direction: Read the words and make a sentence.

bed	led	red	wed
łóżko	prowadzący	czerwony	ślub

Name _______________________

Draw a Picture

I Can...

- [ ] use a Capital Letter
  The cat is big.

- [ ] use spaces

- [ ] sound out words
  d-o-g = dog

- [ ] use a Period .

- [ ] Draw a picture

Name: __________________ Date: __________

Today is: Monday   Tuesday   Wednesday
           Thursday   Friday

Name: ___________________ Date: ___________________

Today is: [Monday] [Tuesday] [Wednesday]
          [Thursday] [Friday]

Direction: Read the words and make a sentence.

bad	**dad**	**mad**	**sad**
zły	tata	szalony	smutny

Name ______________________________

<table>
<tr><td>

Draw a Picture

</td><td>

I Can...

☐ use a Capital Letter
The cat is big.

☐ use spaces

☐ sound out words
d-o-g = dog

☐ use a Period .

☐ Draw a
picture

</td></tr>
</table>

Name: _______________________   Date: _______________

Today is: Monday Tuesday Wednesday Thursday Friday

Direction: Read the words and make a sentence.

den	hen	pen	ten
legowisko	kura	stajnie	dziesięć

Name

Draw a Picture

I Can...

- [ ] use a Capital Letter
The cat is big.

- [ ] use spaces

- [ ] sound out words
d-o-g = dog

- [ ] use a Period .

- [ ] Draw a picture

Name: ___________________   Date: ___________________

Today is: | Monday | Tuesday | Wednesday |
| Thursday | Friday |

Name: __________________ Date: __________________

Today is: [Monday] [Tuesday] [Wednesday]
[Thursday] [Friday]

Direction: Read the words and make a sentence.

gum	mum	sum	drum
lepki	milczący	suma	bęben

Name

Draw a Picture

I Can...

☐ use a Capital Letter
The cat is big.

☐ use spaces

☐ sound out words
d-o-g = dog

☐ use a Period .

☐ Draw a picture

Name: _______________________ Date: _______________________

Today is: Monday Tuesday Wednesday Thursday Friday

Name: _______________________ Date: _______________________

Today is: [Monday] [Tuesday] [Wednesday]
[Thursday] [Friday]

Direction: Read the words and make a sentence.

bid	**hid**	**kid**	**lid**
stawka	ukryć	dziecko	pokrywa

____

____

____

____

____

Name

Draw a Picture

I Can...

- [ ] use a Capital Letter
  The cat is big.

- [ ] use spaces

- [ ] sound out words
  d-o-g = dog

- [ ] use a Period .

- [ ] Draw a
  picture

Name: _______________________ Date: _______________

Today is: Monday Tuesday Wednesday Thursday Friday

Name: _________________ Date: _________________

Today is: Monday Tuesday Wednesday Thursday Friday

Direction: Read the words and make a sentence.

big	**dig**	**pig**	**wig**
duży	kopać	świnia	peruka

Name ___________________________

<table>
<tr><td>

Draw a Picture

</td><td>

I Can...

☐ use a Capital Letter
The cat is big.

☐ use spaces

☐ sound out words
d-o-g = dog

☐ use a Period .

☐ Draw a picture

</td></tr>
</table>

Name: _________________________ Date: _________________

Today is: Monday Tuesday Wednesday Thursday Friday

Name: ______________________ Date: ______________________

Today is: Monday | Tuesday | Wednesday | Thursday | Friday

Direction: Read the words and make a sentence.

bin	fin	pin	win
	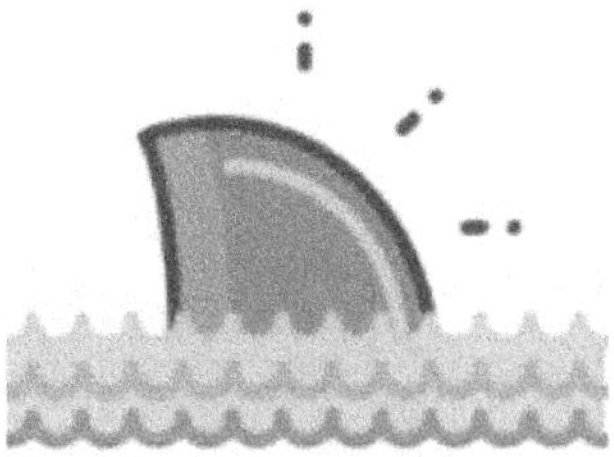		
kosz	płetwa	kołek	zdobyć

____

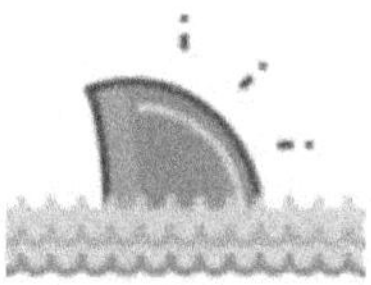

____

____

____

Name

Draw a Picture

I Can...

- [ ] use a Capital Letter
  The cat is big.

- [ ] use spaces

- [ ] sound out words
  d-o-g = dog

- [ ] use a Period .

- [ ] Draw a picture

Name: _______________________ Date: _______________________

Today is: [Monday] [Tuesday] [Wednesday]
[Thursday] [Friday]

Name: _________________________ Date: _________________

Today is: [Monday] [Tuesday] [Wednesday] [Thursday] [Friday]

Direction: Read the words and make a sentence.

hip	**lip**	**nip**	**sip**
cześć p	usta	uszczypnięcie	drink

Name ____________________________________

<table>
<tr><td>

Draw a Picture

</td><td>

I Can...

☐ use a Capital Letter
The cat is big.

☐ use spaces

☐ sound out words
d-o-g = dog

☐ use a Period .

☐ Draw a picture

</td></tr>
</table>

Name: _________________________ Date: _________________________

Today is: Monday   Tuesday   Wednesday   Thursday   Friday

Name: _________________________ Date: _________________________

Today is: Monday   Tuesday   Wednesday
          Thursday   Friday

Direction: Read the words and make a sentence.

fit	hit	kit	sit
dopasowanie	trafienie	zestaw	siedzieć

Name

Draw a Picture

I Can...

- ☐ use a Capital Letter
  The cat is big.

- ☐ use spaces

- ☐ sound out words
  d-o-g = dog

- ☐ use a Period .

- ☐ Draw a picture

Name: _________________________ Date: _______________

Today is: Monday Tuesday Wednesday Thursday Friday

Name: _________________ Date: _______________

Today is: Monday Tuesday Wednesday

Thursday Friday

Direction: Read the words and make a sentence.

cob	job	rob	sob
kukurydza	praca	obrabować	płakać

Name

Draw a Picture

I Can...

- [ ] use a Capital Letter
  <u>T</u>he cat is big.

- [ ] use spaces

- [ ] sound out words
  d-o-g = dog

- [ ] use a Period .

- [ ] Draw a picture

Name: _________________ Date: _________________

Today is: Monday | Tuesday | Wednesday
Thursday | Friday

Name: _______________________ Date: _______________________

Today is: [Monday] [Tuesday] [Wednesday]
[Thursday] [Friday]

Direction: Read the words and make a sentence.

dog	hog	jog	log
pies	wieprz	jogging	drewno

Name

Draw a Picture

I Can...

- [ ] use a Capital Letter
  The cat is big.

- [ ] use spaces

- [ ] sound out words
  d-o-g = dog

- [ ] use a Period .

- [ ] Draw a picture

Name: _________________________ Date: _______________

Today is: Monday Tuesday Wednesday Thursday Friday

Name: _________________________ Date: _______________

Today is: [Monday] [Tuesday] [Wednesday]
[Thursday] [Friday]

Direction: Read the words and make a sentence.

bug	**hug**	**jug**	**mug**
pluskwa	przytulić	dzbanek	kubek

Name

Draw a Picture

I Can...

- [ ] use a Capital Letter
  The cat is big.

- [ ] use spaces

- [ ] sound out words
  d-o-g = dog

- [ ] use a Period .

- [ ] Draw a picture

Name: _______________________   Date: _______________________

Today is: Monday Tuesday Wednesday Thursday Friday

Name: ___________________ Date: ___________________

Today is: Monday Tuesday Wednesday Thursday Friday

Direction: Read the words and make a sentence.

cot	dot	hot	pot
łóżko	kropka	gorąco	garnek

Name

Draw a Picture

I Can...

- [ ] use a Capital Letter
  The cat is big.

- [ ] use spaces

- [ ] sound out words
  d-o-g = dog

- [ ] use a Period .

- [ ] Draw a picture

Name: _____________________ Date: _____________________

Today is: Monday Tuesday Wednesday
Thursday Friday